Dishcloth #1

Shown on Front Cover.

Finished Size: 10³/₄" (27.5 cm) square

MATERIALS

100% Cotton Medium Weight Yarn **(4)** MEDIUM

**[5 ounces, 236 yards
(140 grams, 212 meters) per ball]:**
Yellow - 1 ball
Blue - 1 ball
White - 1 ball
Crochet hook, size G (4 mm) **or** size needed
for gauge

GAUGE SWATCH: 2" (5 cm) square
Work same as Body for 2 rnds.

STITCH GUIDE

> **CLUSTER**
> Ch 2, dc in second ch from hook.

BODY

Rnd 1: With Yellow, ch 2, sc in second ch from hook, (ch 3, sc in same ch) 3 times, ch 1, hdc in first sc to form last ch-3 sp: 4 sc and 4 ch-3 sps.

Rnd 2 (Right side): Ch 1, turn; sc in last ch-3 sp made, work Cluster, ★ (sc, ch 5, sc) in next ch-3 sp, work Cluster; repeat from ★ 2 times **more**, sc in same sp as first sc, ch 2, dc in first sc to form last ch-5 sp: 4 Clusters and 4 ch-5 sps.

Note: Loop a short piece of yarn around any sc to mark Rnd 2 as **right** side.

Rnd 3: Ch 1, turn; sc in last ch-5 sp made, work Cluster, sc in next Cluster (ch-1 sp), work Cluster, ★ (sc, ch 5, sc) in next ch-5 sp, work Cluster, sc in next Cluster, work Cluster; repeat from ★ 2 times **more**, sc in same sp as first sc, ch 2, dc in first sc to form last ch-5 sp: 8 Clusters and 4 ch-5 sps.

Rnds 4-9: Ch 1, work Cluster, (sc in next Cluster, work Cluster) across to next ch-5 ch-5 sp, work Cluster, (sc in next Cluster, work Cluster) across to next ch-5 sp; repeat from ★ 2 times **more**, sc in same sp as first sc, ch 2, dc in first sc to form last ch-5 sp: 32 Clusters and 4 ch-5 sps.

Rnd 10: Ch 1, turn; sc in last ch-5 sp made, work Cluster, (sc in next Cluster, work Cluster) across to next ch-5 sp, ★ (sc, ch 5, sc) in next ch-5 sp, work Cluster, (sc in next Cluster, work Cluster) across to next ch-5 sp; repeat from ★ 2 times **more**, sc in same sp as first sc, ch 5; join with slip st to first sc, finish off: 36 Clusters and 4 ch-5 sps.

Rnd 11: With **wrong** side facing, join Blue with sc in any ch-5 sp *(see Joining With Sc, page 28)*; ch 3, sc in same sp, ch 2, ★ (sc in next Cluster, ch 2) across to next ch-5 sp, (sc, ch 3, sc) in ch-5 sp, ch 2; repeat from ★ 2 times **more**, (sc in next Cluster, ch 2) across; join with slip st to first sc, finish off: 44 sc and 44 sps.

Rnd 12: With **right** side facing, join White with dc in any ch-3 sp *(see Joining With Dc, page 28)*; (dc, ch 3, 2 dc) in same sp, ch 1, ★ (2 dc in next ch-2 sp, ch 1) across to next ch-3 sp, (2 dc, ch 3, 2 dc) in ch-3 sp, ch 1; repeat from ★ 2 times **more**, (dc in next ch-2 sp, ch 1) across; join with slip st to first dc, finish off: 96 sc and 48 sps.

Rnd 13: With **wrong** side facing, join Blue with sc in any ch-3 sp; ch 3, sc in same sp, ch 2, ★ (sc in next ch-1 sp, ch 2) across to next ch-3 sp, (sc, ch 3, sc) in ch-3 sp, ch 2; repeat from ★ 2 times **more**, (sc in next ch-1 sp, ch 2) across; join with slip st to first sc, do **not** finish off: 52 sc and 52 sps.

Rnd 14: Ch 2, turn; dc in same st, ★ (slip, ch 2, dc) in each sc across to next ch-3 sp, (slip st, ch 2, dc) in center ch of next ch-3; repeat from ★ 2 times **more**; join with slip st to joining slip st, finish off.

Dishcloth #2

Shown on Front Cover.

◀■■■◻ INTERMEDIATE

Finished Size: 10¼" (26 cm) square

MATERIALS

100% Cotton Medium Weight Yarn (MEDIUM 4)
[5 ounces, 236 yards
(140 grams, 212 meters) per ball]:
White - 1 ball
Blue - 1 ball
Yellow - 1 ball
Crochet hook, size G (4 mm) **or** size needed
for gauge

GAUGE SWATCH: 2¾" (7 cm) square
Work same as Dishcloth for 2 rnds.

STITCH GUIDE

BEGINNING CLUSTER (uses first 3 sts)
Ch 2, ★ YO, insert hook in **next** dc, YO and
pull up a loop, YO and draw through 2 loops
on hook; repeat from ★ once **more**, YO and
draw through all 3 loops on hook.

CLUSTER (uses next 3 dc)
★ YO, insert hook in **next** dc, YO and pull up
a loop, YO and draw through 2 loops on hook;
repeat from ★ 2 times **more**, YO and draw
through all 4 loops on hook.

PICOT
Ch 3, YO, insert hook in third ch from hook,
YO and pull up a loop, YO and draw through
2 loops on hook, YO, insert hook in **same** ch,
YO and pull up a loop, YO and draw through
2 loops on hook, YO and draw through all
3 loops on hook.

DISHCLOTH

Rnd 1 (Wrong side)**:** With Blue, ch 4, 2 dc in fourth
ch from hook **(3 skipped chs count as first dc)**,
ch 3, (3 dc in same ch, ch 3) 3 times; join with slip st
to first dc, finish off: 12 dc and 4 ch-3 sps.

Note: Loop a short piece of yarn around **back** of
any dc on Rnd 1 to mark **right** side.

Rnd 2: With **right** side facing, join White with dc in
any ch-3 sp *(see Joining With Dc, page 28)*; (2 dc,
ch 3, 3 dc) in same sp, ch 1, ★ (3 dc, ch 3, 3 dc) in
next ch-3 sp, ch 1; repeat from ★ 2 times **more**; join
with slip st to first dc, finish off: 24 dc and 8 sps.

Rnd 3: With **wrong** side facing, join Yellow with dc in any ch-3 sp; (2 dc, ch 3, 3 dc) in same sp, ch 1, 3 dc in next ch-1 sp, ch 1, ★ (3 dc, ch 3, 3 dc) in next ch-3 sp, ch 1, 3 dc in next ch-1 sp, ch 1; repeat from ★ 2 times **more**; join with slip st to first dc, finish off: 36 dc and 12 sps.

Rnd 4: With **right** side facing, join White with dc in any ch-3 sp; (2 dc, ch 3, 3 dc) in same sp, ch 1, (3 dc in next ch-1 sp, ch 1) twice, ★ (3 dc, ch 3, 3 dc) in next ch-3 sp, ch 1, (3 dc in next ch-1 sp, ch 1) twice; repeat from ★ 2 times **more**; join with slip st to first dc, finish off: 48 dc and 16 sps.

Rnd 5: With **wrong** side facing, join Blue with dc in any ch-3 sp; (2 dc, ch 3, 3 dc) in same sp, ch 1, ★ (3 dc in next ch-1 sp, ch 1) across to next ch-3 sp, (3 dc, ch 3, 3 dc) in ch-3 sp, ch 1; repeat from ★ 2 times **more**, (3 dc in next ch-1 sp, ch 1) across; join with slip st to first dc, finish off: 60 dc and 20 sps.

Rnd 6: With **right** side facing, join Yellow with dc in any ch-3 sp; (2 dc, ch 3, 3 dc) in same sp, ch 1, ★ (3 dc in next ch-1 sp, ch 1) across to next ch-3 sp, (3 dc, ch 3, 3 dc) in ch-3 sp, ch 1; repeat from ★ 2 times **more**, (3 dc in next ch-1 sp, ch 1) across; join with slip st to first dc, finish off: 72 dc and 24 sps.

Rnd 7: With **wrong** side facing, join Blue with dc in any ch-3 sp; (2 dc, ch 3, 3 dc) in same sp, ch 1, ★ (3 dc in next ch-1 sp, ch 1) across to next ch-3 sp, (3 dc, ch 3, 3 dc) in ch-3 sp, ch 1; repeat from ★ 2 times **more**, (3 dc in next ch-1 sp, ch 1) across; join with slip st to first dc, finish off: 84 dc and 28 sps.

Rnd 8: With **right** side facing, join White with dc in any ch-3 sp; (2 dc, ch 3, 3 dc) in same sp, ch 1, ★ (3 dc in next ch-1 sp, ch 1) across to next ch-3 sp, (3 dc, ch 3, 3 dc) in ch-3 sp, ch 1; repeat from ★ 2 times **more**, (3 dc in next ch-1 sp, ch 1) across; join with slip st to first dc, do **not** finish off: 96 dc and 32 sps.

Rnd 9: Do **not** turn; work Beginning Cluster, work Picot, (dc, work Picot) twice in next ch-3 sp, ★ (work Cluster, work Picot) 8 times, (dc, work Picot) twice in next ch-3 sp; repeat from ★ 2 times **more**, (work Cluster, work Picot) across: join with slip st to Beginning Cluster, finish off.

Dishcloth #3

Shown on Front Cover.

■■■□ INTERMEDIATE

Finished Size: 10" (25.5 cm) square

MATERIALS

100% Cotton Medium Weight Yarn **(4)** MEDIUM
[5 ounces, 236 yards
(140 grams, 212 meters) per ball]:
Blue - 1 ball
Red - 1 ball
White - 1 ball
Crochet hook, size G (4 mm) **or** size needed
for gauge

GAUGE SWATCH: 3" (7.5 cm) square
Work same as Dishcloth for 4 rnds.

STITCH GUIDE

> **TREBLE CROCHET (abbreviated tr)**
> YO twice, insert hook in sp indicated, YO and
> pull up a loop (4 loops on hook), (YO and draw
> through 2 loops on hook) 3 times.

DISHCLOTH

Rnd 1 (Right side): With Red, ch 4, dc in fourth
ch from hook **(3 skipped chs count as first dc)**,
ch 3, (3 dc in same ch, ch 3) 3 times, dc in same
ch; join with slip st to first dc: 12 dc and 4 ch-3 sps.

Note: Loop a short piece of yarn around any dc to
mark Rnd 1 as **right** side.

Rnd 2: Ch 1, turn; sc in same st, ch 1, (sc, ch 3,
sc) in next ch-3 sp, ch 1, ★ skip next dc, sc in next
dc, ch 1, (sc, ch 3, sc) in next ch-3 sp, ch 1; repeat
from ★ 2 times **more**; join with slip st to first sc:
12 sc and 12 sps.

Rnd 3: Ch 1, turn; sc in same st, ch 1, sc in next
sc, ch 5, sc in next sc, ★ (ch 1, sc in next sc) twice,
ch 5, sc in next sc; repeat from ★ 2 times **more**,
ch 1; join with slip st to first sc.

Rnd 4: Ch 1, turn; sc in same st, ch 1, sc in next
sc, ch 1, (sc, ch 3, sc) in next ch-5 sp, ★ (ch 1, sc in
next sc) 3 times, ch 1, (sc, ch 3, sc) in next ch-5 sp;
repeat from ★ 2 times **more**, ch 1, sc in last sc,
ch 1; join with slip st to first sc, finish off.

Rnd 5: With **right** side facing, join White with
sc in second sc **before** any ch-3 sp *(see Joining
With Sc, page 28)*; ★ † working in **front** of
previous rnds, tr in ch-3 sp two rnds **below** next
ch-1, sc in next sc, ch 5, sc in next sc, working
in **front** of previous rnds, tr in same sp as last tr
made, (sc in next sc, ch 1) twice †, sc in next sc;
repeat from ★ 2 times **more**, then repeat from
† to † once; join with slip st to first sc: 28 sts and
12 sps.

Rnd 6: Ch 1, turn; sc in same st, ch 1, ★ (skip next
st, sc in next sc, ch 1) across to next ch-5 sp, (sc,
ch 3, sc) in ch-5 sp, ch 1, sc in next sc, ch 1; repeat
from ★ around; join with slip st to first sc, finish off:
28 sc and 28 sps.

Rnd 7: With **right** side facing, join Blue with sc in second sc **before** any ch-3 sp; ★ † working in **front** of previous rnds, tr in ch-3 sp two rnds **below** next ch-1, sc in next sc, ch 5, sc in next sc, working in **front** of previous rnds, tr in same sp as last tr made, (sc in next sc, ch 1) 4 times †, sc in next sc; repeat from ★ 2 times **more**, then repeat from † to † once; join with slip st to first sc: 36 sts and 20 sps.

Rnd 8: Repeat Rnd 6: 36 sc and 36 sps.

Rnd 9: With **right** side facing, join White with sc in second sc **before** any ch-3 sp; ★ † working in **front** of previous rnds, tr in ch-3 sp two rnds **below** next ch-1, sc in next sc, ch 5, sc in next sc, working in **front** of previous rnds, tr in same sp as last tr made, (sc in next sc, ch 1) 6 times †, sc in next sc; repeat from ★ 2 times **more**, then repeat from † to † once; join with slip st to first sc: 44 sts and 28 sps.

Rnd 10: Repeat Rnd 6: 44 sc and 44 sps.

Rnd 11: With **right** side facing, join Red with sc in second sc **before** any ch-3 sp; ★ † working in **front** of previous rnds, tr in ch-3 sp two rnds **below** next ch-1, sc in next sc, ch 5, sc in next sc, working in **front** of previous rnds, tr in same sp as last tr made, (sc in next sc, ch 1) 8 times †, sc in next sc; repeat from ★ 2 times **more**, then repeat from † to † once; join with slip st to first sc: 52 sts and 36 sps.

Rnd 12: Repeat Rnd 6: 52 sc and 52 sps.

Rnd 13: With **right** side facing, join White with sc in second sc **before** any ch-3 sp; ★ † working in **front** of previous rnds, tr in ch-3 sp two rnds **below** next ch-1, sc in next sc, ch 5, sc in next sc, working in **front** of previous rnds, tr in same sp as last tr made, (sc in next sc, ch 1) 10 times †, sc in next sc; repeat from ★ 2 times **more**, then repeat from † to † once; join with slip st to first sc: 60 sts and 44 sps.

Rnd 14: Repeat Rnd 6: 60 sc and 60 sps.

Rnd 15: With **right** side facing, join Blue with sc in second sc **before** any ch-3 sp; ★ † working in **front** of previous rnds, tr in ch-3 sp two rnds **below** next ch-1, sc in next sc, ch 5, sc in next sc, working in **front** of previous rnds, tr in same sp as last tr made, (sc in next sc, ch 1) 12 times †, sc in next sc; repeat from ★ 2 times **more**, then repeat from † to † once; join with slip st to first sc: 68 sts and 52 sps.

Rnd 16: Repeat Rnd 6: 68 sc and 68 sps.

Rnd 17: With **right** side facing, join White with sc in second sc **before** any ch-3 sp; ★ † working in **front** of previous rnds, tr in ch-3 sp two rnds **below** next ch-1, sc in next sc, ch 5, sc in next sc, working in **front** of previous rnds, tr in same sp as last tr made, (sc in next sc, ch 1) 14 times †, sc in next sc; repeat from ★ 2 times **more**, then repeat from † to † once; join with slip st to first sc: 76 sts and 60 sps.

Rnd 18: Ch 1, do **not** turn; ★ sc in next tr, ch 1, skip next sc, (sc, ch 1) 4 times in next ch-4 sp, skip next sc, sc in next tr, ch 1, skip next sc, (sc in next ch-1 sp, ch 1) 14 times, skip next st; repeat from ★ around; join with slip st to first sc: 80 sc and 80 sps.

Rnd 19: (Slip st in next ch-1 sp, ch 1) around; join with slip st to first slip st, finish off.

Dishcloth #4

Shown on page 14.

Finished Size: 10" (25.5 cm) square

MATERIALS

100% Cotton Medium Weight Yarn 🧶 **4**
[5 ounces, 236 yards
(140 grams, 212 meters) per ball**]:**
1 ball
Crochet hook, size G (4 mm) **or** size needed
for gauge

GAUGE SWATCH: 3" (7.5 cm) square
Work same as Dishcloth for 2 rnds.

STITCH GUIDE

TREBLE CROCHET *(abbreviated tr)*
YO twice, insert hook in st indicated, YO and
pull up a loop (4 loops on hook), (YO and draw
through 2 loops on hook) 3 times.
CROSS ST *(uses next 3 sts)*
Skip next 2 sts, dc in next st, ch 1, working
behind dc just made, tr in first skipped st.

DISHCLOTH

Rnd 1 (Right side)**:** Ch 4, 2 dc in fourth ch
from hook **(3 skipped chs count as first dc)**,
(ch 3, 3 dc in same ch) 3 times, ch 1, hdc in first dc
to form last ch-3 sp: 12 dc and 4 ch-3 sps.

Rnd 2: Ch 3 **(counts as first dc, now and throughout)**, turn; dc in last ch-3 sp made, work Cross St, ★ (2 dc, ch 3, 2 dc) in next ch-3 sp, work Cross St; repeat from ★ 2 times **more**, 2 dc in same sp as first dc, ch 1, hdc in first dc to form last ch-3 sp: 4 Cross Sts and 4 ch-3 sps.

Rnd 3: Ch 3, turn; dc in last ch-3 sp made, work Cross St, sc in next ch-1 sp, work Cross St, ★ (2 dc, ch 3, 2 dc) in next ch-3 sp, work Cross St, sc in next ch-1 sp, work Cross St; repeat from ★ 2 times **more**, 2 dc in same sp as first dc, ch 1, hdc in first dc to form last ch-3 sp: 8 Cross Sts.

Rnds 4-7: Ch 3, turn; dc in last ch-3 sp made, work Cross St, (sc in next ch-1 sp, work Cross St) across to next ch-3 sp, ★ (2 dc, ch 3, 2 dc) in next ch-3 sp, work Cross St, (sc in next ch-1 sp, work Cross St) across to next ch-3 sp; repeat from ★ 2 times **more**, 2 dc in same sp as first dc, ch 1, hdc in first dc to form last ch-3 sp: 28 sps.

Rnd 8: Ch 3, turn; dc in last ch-3 sp made, work Cross St, (sc in next ch-1 sp, work Cross St) across to next ch-3 sp, ★ (2 dc, ch 3, 2 dc) in next ch-3 sp, work Cross St, (sc in next ch-1 sp, work Cross St) across to next ch-3 sp; repeat from ★ 2 times **more**, 2 dc in same sp as first dc, ch 3; join with slip st to first dc: 32 sps.

Rnd 9: Ch 4 **(counts as first dc plus ch 1)**, turn; ★ † (dc, ch 1) 4 times in next ch-3 sp, dc in next dc, (dc, ch 1, dc) in next 7 ch-1 sps, skip next 2 dc †, dc in next dc, ch 1; repeat from ★ 2 times **more**, then repeat from † to † once; join with slip st to first dc: 48 ch-1 sps

Rnd 10: Do **not** turn; (slip st, ch 2, dc) in each ch-1 sp around; join with slip st to first slip st, finish off.

Dishcloth #5

Shown on page 14.

◼◼◼◻ INTERMEDIATE

Finished Size: 9³/₄" (25 cm) square

MATERIALS
100% Cotton Medium Weight Yarn 🄬
[4 ounces, 189 yards
(113 grams, 170 meters) per ball]:
Variegated - 1 ball
[5 ounces, 236 yards
(140 grams, 212 meters) per ball]:
White - 1 ball
Crochet hook, size G (4 mm) **or** size needed
for gauge

GAUGE SWATCH: 2" (5 cm) square
Work same as Dishcloth for 3 rnds.

DISHCLOTH
Rnd 1 (Right side): With Variegated, ch 2, sc in second ch from hook, ch 2, (sc in same ch, ch 2) 3 times; join with slip st to first sc: 4 sc and 4 ch-2 sps.

Note: Loop a short piece of yarn around any sc to mark Rnd 1 as **right** side.

Rnd 2: Ch 1, turn; ★ (sc, ch 3, sc) in next ch-2 sp, dc in next sc; repeat from ★ around; join with slip st to first sc: 12 sts and 4 ch-3 sps.

Rnd 3: Ch 1, turn; ★ sc in next dc, dc in next sc, (sc, ch 3, sc) in next ch-3 sp, dc in next sc; repeat from ★ 3 times **more**; join with slip st to first sc: 20 sts and 4 ch-3 sps.

Rnd 4: Ch 1, turn; sc in next dc, dc in next sc, (sc, ch 3, sc) in next ch-3 sp, ★ dc in next sc, (sc in next dc, dc in next sc) twice, (sc, ch 3, sc) in next ch-3 sp; repeat from ★ 2 times **more**, dc in next sc, sc in next dc, dc in last sc; join with slip st to first sc: 28 sts and 4 ch-3 sps.

Rnd 5: Ch 1, turn; (sc in next dc, dc in next sc) twice, (sc, ch 3, sc) in next ch-3 sp, ★ dc in next sc, (sc in next dc, dc in next sc) 3 times, (sc, ch 3, sc) in next ch-3 sp; repeat from ★ 2 times **more**, dc in next sc, sc in next dc, dc in last sc; join with slip st to first sc: 36 sts and 4 ch-3 sps.

Rnds 6-14: Ch 1, turn; ★ (sc in next dc, dc in next sc) across to next ch-3 sp, (sc, ch 3, sc) in ch-3 sp, dc in next sc; repeat from ★ 3 times **more**, (sc in next dc, dc in next sc) across; join with slip st to first sc: 108 sts and 4 ch-3 sps.

Finish off.

Rnd 15: With **right** side facing, join White with sc in center dc on any side *(see Joining With Sc, page 28)*; ★ ch 1, skip next sc, (sc in next dc, ch 1, skip next sc) across to next ch-3 sp, (sc, ch 3, sc) in ch-3 sp; repeat from ★ 3 times **more**, ch 1, skip next sc, (sc in next dc, ch 1, skip next sc) across; join with slip st to first sc: 60 sc and 60 sps.

Rnd 16: Do **not** turn; ★ (slip st in next ch-1 sp, ch 1, hdc in next sc) across to next ch-3 sp, slip st in next ch-3 sp, ch 1, hdc in center ch, ch 1, slip st in same sp, ch 1, hdc in next sc; repeat from ★ 3 times **more**, (slip st in next ch-1 sp, ch 1, hdc in next sc) across; join with slip st to first slip st, finish off.

Dishcloth #6

Shown on page 14.

■■■□ INTERMEDIATE

Finished Size: 10¹/₄" (26 cm) square

MATERIALS
100% Cotton Medium Weight Yarn **4**
[5 ounces, 236 yards
(140 grams, 212 meters) per ball**]**:
Ecru - 1 ball
Red - 1 ball
Blue - 1 ball
Crochet hook, size G (4 mm) **or** size needed
for gauge
Safety pin

GAUGE SWATCH: 2" (5 cm) square
Work same as Dishcloth for 2 rnds.

DISHCLOTH

Rnd 1 (Right side)**:** With Ecru, ch 4, 2 dc in fourth ch from hook **(3 skipped chs count as first dc)**, ch 3, (3 dc in same ch, ch 3) 3 times; join with slip st to first dc, place loop from hook onto safety pin to prevent rnd from unraveling: 12 dc and 4 ch-3 sps.

Note: Loop a short piece of yarn around any dc to mark Rnd 1 as **right** side.

Rnd 2: With **wrong** side facing and keeping loop to **wrong** side of work, join Red with sc in any ch-3 sp *(see Joining With Sc, page 28)*; ch 3, sc in same sp, ch 1, skip next dc, sc in next dc, ch 1, ★ (sc, ch 3, sc) in next ch-3 sp, ch 1, skip next dc, sc in next dc, ch 1; repeat from ★ 2 times **more**; join with slip st to first sc, finish off: 12 sc and 12 sps.

Rnd 3: With **right** side facing, place loop from safety pin onto hook, ch 3 **(counts as first dc, now and throughout)**, sc in next sc, working **behind** next ch-1, dc in skipped dc one rnd **below** ch-1, sc in next sc, ch 4, sc in next sc, ★ (working **behind** next ch-1, dc in skipped dc one rnd **below** ch-1, sc in next sc) twice, ch 4, sc in next sc; repeat from ★ 2 times **more**; join with slip st to first dc, place loop from hook onto safety pin to prevent rnd from unraveling: 20 sts and 4 ch-4 sps.

Rnd 4: With **wrong** side facing and keeping loop to **wrong** side of work, join Blue with sc in sc **before** any corner ch-4 sp; ch 1, (sc, ch 3, sc) in ch-4 sp, ch 1, ★ sc in next sc, ch 1, (skip next dc, sc in next sc, ch 1) across to next ch-4 sp, (sc, ch 3, sc) in ch-4 sp, ch 1; repeat from ★ 2 times **more**, (sc in next sc, ch 1, skip next dc) across; join with slip st to first sc, finish off: 20 sc and 20 sps.

Rnd 5: With **right** side facing, place loop from safety pin onto hook, ch 3, sc in next sc, working **behind** next ch-1, dc in skipped dc one rnd **below** ch-1, sc in next sc, ★ † working **behind** next ch-1, dc in ch-4 sp one rnd **below** ch-1 (before first sc), sc in next sc, ch 4, sc in next sc, working **behind** next ch-1, dc in same sp as last dc made (after second sc), sc in next sc †, (working **behind** next ch-1, dc in skipped dc one rnd **below** ch-1, sc in next sc) twice; repeat from ★ 2 times **more**, then repeat from † to † once; join with slip st to first dc, place loop from hook onto safety pin to prevent rnd from unraveling: 36 sts and 4 ch-4 sps.

Rnd 6: With Red, repeat Rnd 4: 28 sc and 28 sps.

Rnd 7: With **right** side facing, place loop from safety pin onto hook, ch 3, sc in next sc, (working **behind** next ch-1, dc in skipped dc one rnd **below** ch-1, sc in next sc) twice, ★ † working **behind** next ch-1, dc in ch-4 sp one rnd **below** ch-1, sc in next sc, ch 4, sc in next sc, working **behind** next ch-1, dc in same sp as last dc made, sc in next sc †, (working **behind** next ch-1, dc in skipped dc one rnd **below** ch-1, sc in next sc) 4 times; repeat from ★ 2 times **more**, then repeat from † to † once, working **behind** next ch-1, dc in skipped dc one rnd **below** ch-1, sc in last sc; join with slip st to first dc, place loop from hook onto safety pin to prevent rnd from unraveling: 52 sts and 4 ch-4 sps.

Rnd 8: Repeat Rnd 4: 36 sc and 36 sps.

Rnd 9: With **right** side facing, place loop from safety pin onto hook, ch 3, sc in next sc, (working **behind** next ch-1, dc in skipped dc one rnd **below** ch-1, sc in next sc) across to within one ch-1 sp of next corner ch-4 sp, ★ † working **behind** next ch-1, dc in ch-4 sp one rnd **below** ch-1, sc in next sc, ch 4, sc in next sc, working **behind** next ch-1, dc in same sp as last dc made, sc in next sc †, (working **behind** next ch-1, dc in skipped dc one rnd **below** ch-1, sc in next sc) across to within one ch-1 sp of next corner ch-4 sp; repeat from ★ 2 times **more**, then repeat from † to † once, (working **behind** next ch-1, dc in skipped dc one rnd **below** ch-1, sc in next sc) across; join with slip st to first dc, place loop from hook onto safety pin to prevent rnd from unraveling: 68 sts and 4 ch-4 sps.

Rnd 10: With Red, repeat Rnd 4: 44 sc and 44 sps.

Rnd 11: Repeat Rnd 9: 84 sts and 4 ch-4 sps.

Rnd 12: Repeat Rnd 4: 52 sc and 52 sps.

Rnd 13: Repeat Rnd 9: 100 sts and 4 ch-4 sps.

Rnd 14: With Red, repeat Rnd 4: 60 sc and 60 sps.

Rnd 15: Repeat Rnd 9: 116 sts and 4 ch-4 sps.

Rnd 16: Repeat Rnd 4: 68 sc and 68 sps.

Rnd 17: Repeat Rnd 9; do **not** place loop onto safety pin after joining: 132 sts and 4 ch-4 sps.

Rnd 18: Ch 1, do **not** turn; sc in same st, ch 1, ★ skip next sc, (sc in next dc, ch 1, skip next sc) across to next ch-4 sp, (sc, ch 1) 4 times in ch-4 sp; repeat from ★ 3 times **more**, skip next sc, (sc in next dc, ch 1, skip next sc) across; join with slip st to first sc: 80 sps.

Rnd 19: (Slip st in next ch-1 sp, ch 1) around; join with slip st to first slip st, finish off.

Dishcloth #7

Shown on page 15.

■■■□ INTERMEDIATE

Finished Size: 10" (25.5 cm) square

MATERIALS
100% Cotton Medium Weight Yarn 🪢**4**
 [5 ounces, 236 yards
  (140 grams, 212 meters) per ball**]**:
 Ecru - 1 ball
 Red - 1 ball
 Blue - 1 ball
Crochet hook, size G (4 mm) **or** size needed
 for gauge
Safety pins - 2

GAUGE SWATCH: 2³/₄" (7 cm) square
Work same as Body for 5 rnds.

BODY
Rnd 1 (Right side)**:** With Ecru, ch 2, sc in second
ch from hook, ch 2, (sc in same ch, ch 2) 3 times;
join with slip st to first sc, place loop from hook
onto safety pin to prevent rnd from unraveling:
4 sc and 4 ch-2 sps.

Note #1: Loop a short piece of yarn around any sc
to mark Rnd 1 as **right** side.

Note #2: Always keep loop to **wrong** side of work.

Rnd 2: With **wrong** side facing, join Red with sc in
any ch-2 sp *(see Joining With Sc, page 28)*; ch 2,
sc in same sp, ch 1, ★ (sc, ch 2, sc) in next ch-2 sp,
ch 1; repeat from ★ 2 times **more**; join with slip st to
first sc, place loop from hook onto second safety pin
to prevent rnd from unraveling: 8 sc and 8 sps.

Rnd 3: With **right** side facing, place Ecru loop
from safety pin onto hook, ch 2, sc in first ch-1 sp,
ch 1, (sc, ch 2, sc) in next ch-2 sp, ch 1, ★ sc in
next ch-1 sp, ch 1, (sc, ch 2, sc) in next ch-2 sp,
ch 1; repeat from ★ 2 times **more**; join with slip st
to first sc, place loop from hook onto safety pin to
prevent rnd from unraveling: 12 sc and 12 sps.

Rnd 4: With **wrong** side facing, place Red loop
from safety pin onto hook, ch 2, sc in first
ch-1 sp, ch 1, (sc, ch 2, sc) in next ch-2 sp, ch 1,
★ (sc in next ch-1 sp, ch 1) twice, (sc, ch 2, sc) in
next ch-2 sp, ch 1; repeat from ★ 2 times **more**,
sc in next ch-1 sp, ch 1; join with slip st to first sc,
place loop from hook onto safety pin to prevent
rnd from unraveling: 16 sc and 16 sps.

Rnd 5: With **right** side facing, place Ecru loop from
safety pin onto hook, ch 2, sc in first ch-1 sp, ch 1,
sc in next ch-1 sp, ch 1, (sc, ch 2, sc) in next ch-2 sp,
ch 1, ★ (sc in next ch-1 sp, ch 1) 3 times, (sc, ch 2,
sc) innext ch-2 sp, ch 1; repeat from ★ 2 times **more**,
sc in next ch-1 sp, ch 1; join with slip st to first sc,
place loop from hook onto safety pin to prevent rnd
from unraveling: 20 sc and 20 sps.

Rnd 6: With **wrong** side facing, place Red loop from safety pin onto hook, ch 2, sc in first ch-1 sp, ch 1, sc in next ch-1 sp, ch 1, (sc, ch 2, sc) in next ch-2 sp, ch 1, ★ (sc in next ch-1 sp, ch 1) 4 times, (sc, ch 2, sc) in next ch-2 sp, ch 1; repeat from ★ 2 times **more**, (sc in next ch-1 sp, ch 1) twice; join with slip st to first sc, place loop from hook onto safety pin to prevent rnd from unraveling: 24 sc and 24 sps.

Rnd 7: With **right** side facing, place Ecru loop from safety pin onto hook, ch 2, sc in first ch-1 sp, ch 1, ★ (sc in next ch-1 sp, ch 1) across to next ch-2 sp, (sc, ch 2, sc) in ch-2 sp, ch 1; repeat from ★ 3 times **more**, (sc in next ch-1 sp, ch 1) across; join with slip st to first sc, place loop from hook onto safety pin to prevent rnd from unraveling: 28 sc and 28 sps.

Rnd 8: With **wrong** side facing, place Red loop from safety pin onto hook, ch 2, sc in first ch-1 sp, ch 1, ★ (sc in next ch-1 sp, ch 1) across to next ch-2 sp, (sc, ch 2, sc) in ch-2 sp, ch 1; repeat from ★ 3 times **more**, (sc in next ch-1 sp, ch 1) across; join with slip st to first sc, place loop from hook onto safety pin to prevent rnd from unraveling: 32 sc and 32 sps.

Rnds 9-12: Repeat Rnds 7 and 8 twice; at end of Rnd 12, do **not** place Red loop onto safety pin after joining, finish off Red only: 48 sts and 48 sps.

Rnd 13: With **right** side facing, place Ecru loop from safety pin onto hook, ch 2, sc in first ch-1 sp, ch 1, † (sc in next ch-1 sp, ch 1) across to next ch-2 sp, (sc, ch 2, sc) in ch-2 sp, ch 1 †, (sc in next ch-1 sp, ch 1) 6 times, place marker around last ch-1 made, (sc in next ch-1 sp, ch 1) across to next ch-2 sp, (sc, ch 2, sc) in ch-2 sp, ch 1, repeat from † to † twice, (sc in next ch-1 sp, ch 1) across; join with slip st to first sc, place loop from hook onto safety pin to prevent rnd from unraveling: 52 sc and 52 sps.

Rnd 14: With **wrong** side facing, join Blue with sc in marked ch-1 sp; ch 1, ★ (sc in next ch-1 sp, ch 1) across to next ch-2 sp, (sc, ch 2, sc) in ch-2 sp, ch 1; repeat from ★ 3 times **more**, (sc in next ch-1 sp, ch 1) across; join with slip st to first sc, place loop from hook onto safety pin to prevent rnd from unraveling: 56 sc and 56 sps.

Rnds 15-18: With Ecru and Blue, repeat Rnds 7 and 8 twice; at end of Rnd 18, do **not** place Blue loop onto safety pin after joining, finish off Blue only: 72 sts and 72 sps.

Rnd 19: With **right** side facing, place Ecru loop from safety pin onto hook, ch 2, sc in first ch-1 sp, ch 1, ★ (sc in next ch-1 sp, ch 1) across to next ch-2 sp, (sc, ch 2, sc) in ch-2 sp, ch 1; repeat from ★ 3 times **more**, (sc in next ch-1 sp, ch 1) across; join with slip st to first sc: 76 sc and 76 sps.

Rnd 20: ★ (Slip st in next ch-1 sp, ch 1) across to next ch-2 sp, (slip st, ch 2, slip st) in ch-2 sp, ch 1; repeat from ★ 3 times **more**, (slip st in next ch-1 sp, ch 1) across; join with slip st to first slip st, finish off.

Dishcloth #8

Shown on page 15.

Finished Size: $10^3/_4$" (27.5 cm) square

MATERIALS
100% Cotton Medium Weight Yarn (4)
  [4 ounces, 189 yards
    (113 grams, 170 meters) per ball]:
  Variegated - 1 ball
  [5 ounces, 236 yards
    (140 grams, 212 meters) per ball]:
  Ecru - 1 ball
Crochet hook, size G (4 mm) **or** size needed
  for gauge

GAUGE SWATCH: 2" (5 cm) square
Work same as Body for 2 rnds.

STITCH GUIDE

CLUSTER
Ch 2, dc in second ch from hook.

BODY

Rnd 1: With Variegated, ch 2, sc in second ch from hook, (ch 3, sc in same ch) 3 times, ch 1, hdc in first sc to form last ch-3 sp: 4 sc and 4 ch-3 sps.

Rnd 2 (Right side)**:** Ch 1, turn; sc in last ch-3 sp made, work Cluster, ★ (sc, ch 5, sc) in next ch-3 sp, work Cluster; repeat from ★ 2 times **more**, sc in same sp as first sc, ch 2, dc in first sc to form last ch-5 sp: 4 Clusters and 4 ch-5 sps.

Note: Loop a short piece of yarn around any sc to mark Rnd 2 as **right** side.

Rnd 3: Ch 1, turn; sc in last ch-5 sp made, work Cluster, sc in next Cluster (ch-1 sp), work Cluster, ★ (sc, ch 5, sc) in next ch-5 sp, work Cluster, sc in next Cluster, work Cluster; repeat from ★ 2 times **more**, sc in same sp as first sc, ch 2, dc in first sc to form last ch-5 sp: 8 Clusters and 4 ch-5 sps.

Rnds 4-10: Ch 1, turn; sc in last ch-5 sp made, work Cluster, (sc in next Cluster, work Cluster) across to next ch-5 sp, ★ (sc, ch 5, sc) in next ch-5 sp, work Cluster, (sc in next Cluster, work Cluster) across to next ch-5 sp; repeat from ★ 2 times **more**, sc in same sp as first sc, ch 2, dc in first sc to form last ch-5 sp: 36 Clusters and 4 ch-5 sps.

Rnd 11: Ch 1, turn; sc in last ch-5 sp made, work Cluster, (sc in next Cluster, work Cluster) across to next ch-5 sp, ★ (sc, ch 5, sc) in next ch-5 sp, work Cluster, (sc in next Cluster, work Cluster) across to next ch-5 sp; repeat from ★ 2 times **more**, sc in same sp as first sc, ch 5; join with slip st to first sc, finish off: 40 Clusters and 4 ch-5 sps.

Rnd 12: With **wrong** side facing, join Ecru with sc in any ch-5 sp *(see Joining With Sc, page 28)*; ch 3, sc in same sp, ch 2, ★ (sc in next Cluster, ch 2) across to next ch-5 sp, (sc, ch 3, sc) in ch-5 sp, ch 2; repeat from ★ 2 times **more**, (sc in next Cluster, ch 2) across; join with slip st to first sc: 48 sc and 48 sps.

Rnd 13: Ch 2, turn; dc in same st, (slip st, ch 2, dc) in center ch of next ch-3, ★ (slip, ch 2, dc) in each sc across to next ch-3 sp, (slip st, ch 2, dc) in center ch of next ch-3; repeat from ★ 2 times **more**, (slip, ch 2, dc) in each sc across; join with slip st to joining slip st, finish off.

Dishcloth #9

Shown on page 15.

Finished Size: 10" (25.5 cm) square

MATERIALS

100% Cotton Medium Weight Yarn (MEDIUM 4)
[5 ounces, 236 yards
(140 grams, 212 meters) per ball]:
Ecru - 1 ball
Red - 1 ball
Green - 1 ball
Crochet hook, size G (4 mm) **or** size needed
for gauge

GAUGE SWATCH: $2^3/4$" (7 cm) square
Work same as Dishcloth for 5 rnds.

DISHCLOTH

Rnd 1 (Right side)**:** With Ecru, ch 2, sc in second ch from hook, ch 2, (sc in same ch, ch 2) 3 times; join with slip st to first sc: 4 sc and 4 ch-2 sps.

Note: Loop a short piece of yarn around any sc to mark Rnd 1 as **right** side.

Rnd 2: Ch 1, ★ (sc, ch 2, sc) in next ch-2 sp, ch 1; repeat from ★ around; join with slip st to first sc: 8 sc and 8 sps.

Rnd 3: Ch 1, turn; sc in next ch-1 sp, ch 1, (sc, ch 2, sc) in next ch-2 sp, ch 1, ★ sc in next ch-1 sp, ch 1, (sc, ch 2, sc) in next ch-2 sp, ch 1; repeat from ★ 2 times **more**; join with slip st to first sc, finish off: 12 sc and 12 sps.

Rnd 4: With **right** side facing, join Red with sc in any ch-2 sp *(see Joining With Sc, page 28)*; ch 2, sc in same sp, ch 1, ★ (sc in next ch-1 sp, ch 1) across to next ch-2 sp, (sc, ch 2, sc) in next ch-2 sp, ch 1; repeat from ★ 2 times **more**, (sc in next ch-1 sp, ch 1) across; join with slip st to first sc, finish off: 16 sc and 16 sps.

Rnd 5: With **wrong** side facing, join Green with sc in any ch-2 sp; ch 2, sc in same sp, ch 1, ★ (sc in next ch-1 sp, ch 1) across to next ch-2 sp, (sc, ch 2, sc) in next ch-2 sp, ch 1; repeat from ★ 2 times **more**, (sc in next ch-1 sp, ch 1) across; join with slip st to first sc, finish off: 20 sc and 20 sps.

Rnd 6: With **right** side facing, join Red with sc in any ch-2 sp; ch 2, sc in same sp, ch 1, ★ (sc in next ch-1 sp, ch 1) across to next ch-2 sp, (sc, ch 2, sc) in next ch-2 sp, ch 1; repeat from ★ 2 times **more**, (sc in next ch-1 sp, ch 1) across; join with slip st to first sc, finish off: 24 sc and 24 sps.

Rnd 7: With **wrong** side facing, join Ecru with sc in any ch-2 sp; ch 2, sc in same sp, ch 1, ★ (sc in next ch-1 sp, ch 1) across to next ch-2 sp, (sc, ch 2, sc) in next ch-2 sp, ch 1; repeat from ★ 2 times **more**, (sc in next ch-1 sp, ch 1) across; join with slip st to first sc: 28 sc and 28 sps.

Rnd 8: Ch 1, turn; ★ (sc in next ch-1 sp, ch 1) across to next ch-2 sp, (sc, ch 2, sc) in next ch-2 sp, ch 1; repeat from ★ around; join with slip st to first sc: 32 sc and 32 sps.

Rnd 9: Ch 1, turn; sc in next ch-1 sp, ch 1, (sc, ch 2, sc) in next ch-2 sp, ch 1, ★ (sc in next ch-1 sp, ch 1) across to next ch-2 sp, (sc, ch 2, sc) in next ch-2 sp, ch 1; repeat from ★ 2 times **more**, (sc in next ch-1 sp, ch 1) across; join with slip st to first sc, finish off: 36 sc and 36 sps.

Rnds 10-20: Repeat Rnds 4-9 once, then repeat Rnds 4-8 once **more**: 80 sc and 80 sps.

Rnds 21: Do **not** turn; ★ (slip st in next ch-1 sp, ch 1) across to next ch-2 sp, (slip st, ch 2, slip st) in ch-2 sp, ch 1; repeat from ★ around, slip st in last ch-1 sp, ch 1; join with slip st to joining slip st, finish off.

#6

#4

#5

#10

14

#7

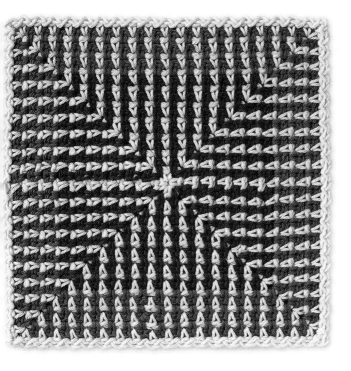

#11

#8

#9

15

Dishcloth #10

Shown on page 14.

■■■◻ INTERMEDIATE

Finished Size: 10" (25.5 cm) square

MATERIALS

100% Cotton Medium Weight Yarn (④ MEDIUM)
[5 ounces, 236 yards
(140 grams, 212 meters) per ball**]**:
Red - 1 ball
Black - 1 ball
White - 1 ball
Crochet hook, size G (4 mm) **or** size needed
for gauge
Safety pin

GAUGE SWATCH: $2^1/2$" (6.25 cm) square
Work same as Dishcloth for 3 rnds.

DISHCLOTH

Rnd 1 (Right side): With Red, ch 4, 2 dc in fourth ch from hook **(3 skipped chs count as first dc)**, ch 3, (3 dc in same ch, ch 3) 3 times; join with slip st to first dc, place loop from hook onto safety pin to prevent rnd from unraveling: 12 dc and 4 ch-3 sps.

Note: Loop a short piece of yarn around any dc to mark Rnd 1 as **right** side.

Rnd 2: With **wrong** side facing and keeping loop to **wrong** side of work, join Black with sc in any ch-3 sp **(see Joining With Sc, page 28)**; ch 3, sc in same sp, ch 1, skip next dc, sc in next dc, ch 1, ★ (sc, ch 3, sc) in next ch-3 sp, ch 1, skip next dc, sc in next dc, ch 1; repeat from ★ 2 times **more**; join with slip st to first sc, finish off: 12 sc and 12 sps.

Rnd 3: With **right** side facing, place loop from safety pin onto hook, ch 3 **(counts as first dc, now and throughout)**, sc in next sc, working **behind** next ch-1, dc in skipped dc one rnd **below** ch-1, sc in next sc, ch 4, sc in next sc, ★ (working **behind** next ch-1, dc in skipped dc one rnd **below** ch-1, sc in next sc) twice, ch 4, sc in next sc; repeat from ★ 2 times **more**; join with slip st to first dc, place loop from hook onto safety pin to prevent rnd from unraveling: 20 sts and 4 ch-4 sps.

Rnd 4: With **wrong** side facing and keeping loop to **right** side of work, join White with sc in sc **before** any corner ch-4 sp; ch 1, (sc, ch 3, sc) in ch-4 sp, ch 1, ★ sc in next sc, ch 1, (skip next dc, sc in next sc, ch 1) across to next ch-4 sp, (sc, ch 3, sc) in ch-4 sp, ch 1; repeat from ★ 2 times **more**, (sc in next sc, ch 1, skip next dc) across; join with slip st to first sc, finish off: 20 sc and 20 sps.

Rnd 5: With **right** side facing, place loop from safety pin onto hook, ch 3, sc in next sc, working **front** of next ch-1, dc in skipped dc one rnd **below** ch-1, sc in next sc, ★ † working **behind** next ch-1, dc in ch-4 sp one rnd **below** ch-1 (before first sc), sc in next sc, ch 4, sc in next sc, working **behind** next ch-1, dc in same sp as last dc made (after second sc), sc in next sc †, (working **front** of next ch-1, dc in skipped dc one rnd **below** ch-1, sc in next sc) twice; repeat from ★ 2 times **more**, then repeat from † to † once; join with slip st to first dc, place loop from hook onto safety pin to prevent rnd from unraveling: 36 sts and 4 ch-4 sps.

Rnd 6: With **wrong** side facing and keeping loop to **wrong** side of work, join Black with sc in sc **before** any corner ch-4 sp; ch 1, (sc, ch 3, sc) in ch-4 sp, ch 1, ★ sc in next sc, ch 1, (skip next dc, sc in next sc, ch 1) across to next ch-4 sp, (sc, ch 3, sc) in ch-4 sp, ch 1; repeat from ★ 2 times **more**, (sc in next sc, ch 1, skip next dc) across; join with slip st to first sc, finish off: 28 sc and 28 sps.

Rnd 7: With **right** side facing, place loop from safety pin onto hook, ch 3, sc in next sc, (working **behind** next ch-1, dc in skipped dc one rnd **below** ch-1, sc in next sc) across to within one ch-1 sp of next corner ch-4 sp, ★ † working **behind** next ch-1, dc in ch-4 sp one rnd **below** ch-1, sc in next sc, ch 4, sc in next sc, working **behind** next ch-1, dc in same sp as last dc made, sc in next sc †, (working **behind** next ch-1, dc in skipped dc one rnd **below** ch-1, sc in next sc) across to within one ch-1 sp of next corner ch-4 sp; repeat from ★ 2 times **more**, then repeat from † to † once, working **behind** next ch-1, dc in skipped dc one rnd **below** ch-1, sc in next sc; join with slip st to first dc, place loop from hook onto safety pin to prevent rnd from unraveling: 52 sts and 4 ch-4 sps.

Rnd 8: Repeat Rnd 4: 36 sc and 36 sps.

Rnd 9: With **right** side facing, place loop from safety pin onto hook, ch 3, sc in next sc, (working **front** of next ch-1, dc in skipped dc one rnd **below** ch-1, sc in next sc) across to within one ch-1 sp of next corner ch-4 sp, ★ † working **behind** next ch-1, dc in ch-4 sp one rnd **below** ch-1, sc in next sc, ch 4, sc in next sc, working **behind** next ch-1, dc in same sp as last dc made, sc in next sc †, (working **front** of next ch-1, dc in skipped dc one rnd **below** ch-1, sc in next sc) across to within one ch-1 sp of next corner ch-4 sp; repeat from ★ 2 times **more**, then repeat from † to † once, (working **front** of next ch-1, dc in skipped dc one rnd **below** ch-1, sc in next sc) across; join with slip st to first dc, place loop from hook onto safety pin to prevent rnd from unraveling: 68 sts and 4 ch-4 sps.

Rnd 10: Repeat Rnd 6: 44 sc and 44 sps.

Rnd 11: With **right** side facing, place loop from safety pin onto hook, ch 3, sc in next sc, (working **behind** next ch-1, dc in skipped dc one rnd **below** ch-1, sc in next sc) across to within one ch-1 sp of next corner ch-4 sp, ★ † working **behind** next ch-1, dc in ch-4 sp one rnd **below** ch-1, sc in next sc, ch 4, sc in next sc, working **behind** next ch-1, dc in same sp as last dc made, sc in next sc †, (working **behind** next ch-1, dc in skipped dc one rnd **below** ch-1, sc in next sc) across to within one ch-1 sp of next corner ch-4 sp; repeat from ★ 2 times **more**, then repeat from † to † once, (working **behind** next ch-1, dc in skipped dc one rnd **below** ch-1, sc in next sc) across; join with slip st to first dc, place loop from hook onto safety pin to prevent rnd from unraveling: 84 sts and 4 ch-4 sps.

Rnd 12: Repeat Rnd 4: 52 sc and 52 sps.

Rnd 13: Repeat Rnd 9: 100 sts and 4 ch-4 sps.

Rnd 14: Repeat Rnd 6: 60 sc and 60 sps.

Rnd 15: Repeat Rnd 11; do **not** place loop onto safety pin after joining: 116 sts and 4 ch-4 sps.

Rnd 16: Ch 1, do **not** turn; sc in first dc, ch 1, ★ skip next sc, (sc in next dc, ch 1, skip next sc) across to next ch-4 sp, (sc, ch 1) 4 times in ch-1 sp; repeat from ★ 3 times **more**, skip next sc, (sc in next dc, ch 1, skip next sc) across; join with slip st to first sc: 72 sps.

Rnd 17: (Slip st in next ch-1 sp, ch 1) around; join with slip st to first slip st, finish off.

Dishcloth #11

Shown on page 15.

Finished Size: 10$\frac{1}{2}$" (26.5 cm) square

MATERIALS
100% Cotton Medium Weight Yarn **④ MEDIUM 4**
  [5 ounces, 236 yards
    (140 grams, 212 meters) per ball**]**:
  Ecru - 1 ball
  Green - 1 ball
  Crochet hook, size G (4 mm) **or** size needed
    for gauge

GAUGE SWATCH: 2" (5 cm) square
Work same as Dishcloth for 2 rnds.

DISHCLOTH

Rnd 1 (Right side)**:** With Ecru, ch 4, dc in fourth ch from hook **(3 skipped chs count as first dc)**, ch 3, (3 dc in same ch, ch 3) 3 times, dc in same ch; join with slip st to first dc: 12 dc and 4 ch-3 sps.

Note: Loop a short piece of yarn around any dc to mark Rnd 1 as **right** side.

Rnd 2: Ch 1, turn; sc in first dc, ch 1, (sc, ch 3, sc) in next ch-3 sp, ch 1, ★ skip next dc, sc in next dc, ch 1, (sc, ch 3, sc) in next ch-3 sp, ch 1; repeat from ★ 2 times **more**; join with slip st to first sc, finish off: 12 sc and 12 sps.

Rnd 3: With **right** side facing, join Green with sc in sc **before** any ch-3 sp *(see Joining With Sc, page 28)*; ch 4, ★ † (sc in next sc, working **behind** next ch-1, dc in skipped dc one rnd **below** ch-1) twice †, sc in next sc, ch 4; repeat from ★ 2 times **more**, then repeat from † to † once; join with slip st to first sc: 20 sts and 4 ch-4 sps.

Rnd 4: Ch 1, turn; sc in first sc, ch 1, (skip next dc, sc in next sc, ch 1) twice, (sc, ch 3, sc) in next ch-4 sp, ch 1, ★ sc in next sc, ch 1, (skip next dc, sc in next sc, ch 1) twice, (sc, ch 3, sc) in next ch-4 sp, ch 1; repeat from ★ 2 times **more**; join with slip st to first sc, finish off: 20 sc and 20 sps.

Rnd 5: With **right** side facing, join Ecru with sc in same st as joining; ★ † working **behind** next ch-1, dc in ch-4 sp one rnd **below** ch-1 (before first sc), sc in next sc, ch 4, sc in next sc, working **behind** next ch-1, dc in same sp as last dc made (after second sc), (sc in next sc, working **behind** next ch-1, dc in skipped dc one rnd **below** ch-1) twice †, sc in next sc; repeat from ★ 2 times **more**, then repeat from † to † once; join with slip st to first sc: 36 sts and 4 ch-4 sps.=

Rnd 6: Ch 1, turn; sc in first sc, ch 1, (skip next dc, sc in next sc, ch 1) 3 times, (sc, ch 3, sc) in next ch-4 sp, ch 1, sc in next sc, ch 1, ★ (skip next dc, sc in next sc, ch 1) 4 times, (sc, ch 3, sc) in next ch-4 sp, ch 1, sc in next sc, ch 1; repeat from ★ 2 times **more**; join with slip st to first sc, finish off: 28 sc and 28 sps.

Rnd 7: With **right** side facing, join Green with sc in fourth sc **before** any ch-3 sp; ★ † (working **behind** next ch-1, dc in skipped dc one rnd **below** ch-1, sc in next sc) across to within one ch-1 sp of next corner ch-4 sp, working **behind** next ch-1, dc in ch-4 sp one rnd **below** ch-1, sc in next sc, ch 4, sc in next sc, working **behind** next ch-1, dc in same sp as last dc made †, sc in next sc; repeat from ★ 2 times **more**, then repeat from † to † once, (sc in next sc, working **behind** next ch-1, dc in skipped dc one rnd **below** ch-1) across; join with slip st to first sc: 52 sts and 4 ch-4 sps.

Rnd 8: Ch 1, turn; sc in first sc, ch 1, ★ (skip next dc, sc in next sc, ch 1) across to next ch-4 sp, (sc, ch 3, sc) in next ch-4 sp, ch 1, sc in next sc, ch 1; repeat from ★ 3 times **more**, (skip next dc, sc in next sc, ch 1) across; join with slip st to first sc, finish off: 36 sc and 36 sps.

Rnds 9 and 10: With Ecru, repeat Rnds 7 and 8: 44 sts and 44 sps.

Rnds 11 and 12: Repeat Rnds 7 and 8: 52 sc and 52 sps.

Rnds 13 and 14: With Ecru, repeat Rnds 7 and 8: 60 sts and 60 sps.

Rnds 15 and 16: Repeat Rnds 7 and 8: 68 sc and 68 sps.

Rnd 17: With Ecru, repeat Rnd 7: 132 sts and 4 ch-4 sps.

Rnd 18: Ch 1, do **not** turn; sc in first dc, ch 1, ★ skip next sc, (sc in next dc, ch 1, skip next sc) across to next ch-4 sp, (sc, ch 1) 4 times in ch-4 sp; repeat from ★ 3 times **more**, skip next sc, (sc in next dc, ch 1, skip next st) across; join with slip st to first sc: 80 sps.

Rnd 19: (Slip st in next ch-1 sp, ch 1) around; join with slip st to first slip st, finish off.

Dishcloth #12

Shown on Back Cover.

◼◼◼◻ INTERMEDIATE

Finished Size: 9³/₄" (25 cm) square

MATERIALS

100% Cotton Medium Weight Yarn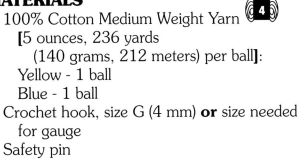

   [5 ounces, 236 yards
     (140 grams, 212 meters) per ball**]:**
   Yellow - 1 ball
   Blue - 1 ball
Crochet hook, size G (4 mm) **or** size needed
   for gauge
Safety pin

GAUGE SWATCH: 2¹/₂" (6.25 cm) square
Work same as Dishcloth for 3 rnds.

STITCH GUIDE

ANCHOR DC
YO, insert hook in back ridge of ch indicated
(Fig. A) **and** in st indicated, YO and draw
through st **and** ch, (YO and draw through
2 loops on hook) twice.

Fig. A

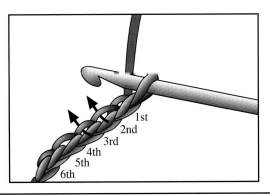

1st
2nd
3rd
4th
5th
6th

DISHCLOTH

Rnd 1 (Right side)**:** With Yellow, ch 4, 2 dc in
fourth ch from hook **(3 skipped chs count as
first dc)**, ch 3, (3 dc in same ch, ch 3) 3 times; join
with slip st to first dc, place loop from hook onto
safety pin to prevent rnd from unraveling: 12 dc
and 4 ch-3 sps.

Note: Loop a short piece of yarn around any dc to
mark Rnd 1 as **right** side.

Rnd 2: With **wrong** side facing and keeping loop
to **right** side of work, join Blue with sc in any
ch-3 sp *(see Joining With Sc, page 28)*; ch 3,
sc in same sp, ch 4, ★ (sc, ch 3, sc) in next ch-3 sp,
ch 4; repeat from ★ 2 times **more**; join with slip st
to first sc, finish off: 8 sc and 8 sps.

Rnd 3: With **right** side facing, place loop from
safety pin onto hook, ch 3 **(counts as first dc,
now and throughout)**, working in **front** of next
ch-4 and in skipped dc one rnd **below** ch-4,
★ † work Anchor dc in third ch of ch-4 and in next
skipped dc *(Fig. A)*, dc in next skipped dc, sc in
next sc, ch 4, sc in next sc †, working in **front** of
next ch-4 and in skipped dc one rnd **below** ch-4,
dc in next skipped dc; repeat from ★ 2 times **more**,
then repeat from † to † once; join with slip st to
first dc, place loop from hook onto safety pin to
prevent rnd from unraveling: 20 sts and 4 ch-4 sps.

Rnd 4: With **wrong** side facing and keeping loop
to **right** side of work, join Blue with sc in any
ch-4 sp; ch 3, sc in same sp, ch 4, skip next 2 sts,
sc in next Anchor dc, ch 4, ★ (sc, ch 3, sc) in next
ch-4 sp, ch 4, skip next 2 sts, sc in next Anchor dc,
ch 4; repeat from ★ 2 times **more**; join with slip st
to first sc, finish off: 12 sc and 12 sps.

20

Rnd 5: With **right** side facing, place loop from safety pin onto hook, ch 3, ★ † sc in next sc, working in **front** of next ch-4 and in skipped sts and ch-3 sp one rnd **below** ch-4, dc in next skipped dc, work Anchor dc in third ch of ch-4 and in next skipped sc, dc in next ch-3 sp (before first sc), sc in next sc, ch 4, sc in next sc, working in **front** of next ch-4 and in skipped ch-3 sp and sts one rnd **below** ch-4, dc in same sp as last dc made (after second sc), work Anchor dc in third ch of ch-4 and in next skipped sc †, dc in next skipped dc; repeat from ★ 2 times **more**, then repeat from † to † once; join with slip st to first dc, place loop from hook onto safety pin to prevent rnd from unraveling: 36 sts and 4 ch-4 sps.

Rnd 6: With **wrong** side facing and keeping loop to **wrong** side of work, join Blue with sc in any ch-4 sp; ch 3, sc in same sp, ch 4, skip next 2 sts, sc in next Anchor dc, (ch 1, skip next dc, sc in next st) twice, ch 4, ★ (sc, ch 3, sc) in next ch-4 sp, ch 4, skip next 2 sts, sc in next Anchor dc, (ch 1, skip next dc, sc in next st) twice, ch 4; repeat from ★ 2 times **more**; join with slip st to first sc, finish off: 20 sc and 20 sps.

Rnd 7: With **right** side facing, place loop from safety pin onto hook, ch 3, sc in next sc, working **behind** next ch-1, dc in skipped dc one rnd **below** ch-1, sc in next sc, ★ † working in **front** of next ch-4 and in skipped sts and ch-3 sp one rnd **below** ch-4, dc in next skipped dc, work Anchor dc in third ch of ch-4 and in next skipped sc, dc in next ch-3 sp, sc in next sc, ch 4, sc in next sc, working in **front** of next ch-4 and in skipped ch-3 sp and sts one rnd **below** ch-4, dc in same sp as last dc made, work Anchor dc in third ch of ch-4 and in next skipped sc, dc in next skipped dc, sc in next sc †, (working **behind** next ch-1, dc in skipped dc one rnd **below** ch-1, sc in next sc) twice; repeat from ★ 2 times **more**, then repeat from † to † once; join with slip st to first dc, place loop from hook onto safety pin to prevent rnd from unraveling: 52 sts and 4 ch-4 sps.

Rnd 8: With **wrong** side facing and keeping loop to **wrong** side of work, join Blue with sc in any ch-4 sp; ch 3, sc in same sp, ch 4, skip next 2 sts, sc in next Anchor dc, (ch 1, skip next dc, sc in next st) across to within 2 sts of next corner ch-4 sp, ch 4, skip next 2 sts, ★ (sc, ch 3, sc) in next ch-4 sp, ch 4, skip next 2 sts, sc in next Anchor dc, (ch 1, skip next dc, sc in next st) across to within 2 sts of next corner ch-4 sp, ch 4, skip next 2 sts; repeat from ★ 2 times **more**; join with slip st to first sc, finish off: 28 sc and 28 sps.

Rnd 9: With **right** side facing, place loop from safety pin onto hook, ch 3, sc in next sc, ★ (working **behind** next ch-1, dc in skipped dc one rnd **below** ch-1, sc in next sc) across to next ch-4 sp, working in **front** of next ch-4 and in skipped sts and ch-3 sp one rnd **below** ch-4, dc in next skipped dc, work Anchor dc in third ch of ch-4 and in next skipped sc, dc in next ch-3 sp, sc in next sc, ch 4, sc in next sc, working in **front** of next ch-4 and in skipped ch-3 sp and sts one rnd **below** ch-4, dc in same sp as last dc made, work Anchor dc in third ch of ch-4 and in next skipped sc, dc in next skipped dc, sc in next sc; repeat from ★ 3 times **more**, working **behind** next ch-1, dc in skipped dc one rnd **below** ch-1, sc in last sc; join with slip st to first dc, place loop from hook onto safety pin to prevent rnd from unraveling: 68 sts and 4 ch-4 sps.

Rnd 10: Repeat Rnd 8: 36 sts and 36 sps.

Rnd 11: With **right** side facing, place loop from safety pin onto hook, ch 3, sc in next sc, ★ (working **behind** next ch-1, dc in skipped dc one rnd **below** ch-1, sc in next sc) across to next ch-4 sp, working in **front** of next ch-4 and in skipped sts and ch-3 sp one rnd **below** ch-4, dc in next skipped dc, work Anchor dc in third ch of ch-4 and in next skipped sc, dc in next ch-3 sp, sc in next sc, ch 4, sc in next sc, working in **front** of next ch-4 and in skipped ch-3 sp and sts one rnd **below** ch-4, dc in same sp as last dc made, work Anchor dc in third ch of ch-4 and in next skipped sc, dc in next skipped dc, sc in next sc; repeat from ★ 3 times **more**, (working **behind** next ch-1, dc in skipped dc one rnd **below** ch-1, sc in next sc) across; join with slip st to first dc, place loop from hook onto safety pin to prevent rnd from unraveling: 84 sts and 4 ch-4 sps.

Instructions continued on page 22.

Rnds 12-15: Repeat Rnds 10 and 11 twice; at end of Rnd 15, do **not** place loop onto safety pin after joining: 116 sts and 4 ch-4 sps.

Rnd 16: Ch 1, do **not** turn; sc in same st, ch 1, ★ skip next sc, (sc in next dc, ch 1, skip next st) across to next ch-4 sp, (sc, ch 1) 4 times in ch-4 sp; repeat from ★ 3 times **more**, skip next sc, (sc in next dc, ch 1, skip next st) across; join with slip st to first sc: 72 ch-1 sps.

Rnd 17: (Slip st in next ch-1 sp, ch 1) around; join with slip st to first slip st, finish off.

Dishcloth #13
Shown on Back Cover.

◼◼◼◻ INTERMEDIATE

Finished Size: 11" (28 cm) square

MATERIALS
100% Cotton Medium Weight Yarn ⓐ④⑨
    [5 ounces, 236 yards
        (140 grams, 212 meters) per ball]:
    Yellow - 2 balls
    Red - 1 ball
    Crochet hook, size G (4 mm) **or** size needed
        for gauge

GAUGE: 11 sts = $2^3/_4$" (7 cm);
            9 rows = $2^1/_4$" (5.75 cm)

Gauge Swatch: $2^3/_4$"w x $2^1/_4$"h
(7 cm x 5.75 cm)
Ch 12.
Work same as Body for 9 rows.
Finish off.

BODY
With Yellow, ch 36.

Row 1: Sc in second ch from hook and in next ch, ch 1, ★ skip next ch, sc in next ch, ch 1; repeat from ★ across to last 3 chs, skip next ch, sc in last 2 chs: 19 sc and 16 ch-1 sps.

Row 2 (Right side)**:** Ch 1, turn; sc in first 2 sc, ch 1, (sc in next sc, ch 1) across to last 2 sc, sc in last 2 sc.

Note: Loop a short piece of yarn around any stitch to mark Row 2 as **right** side.

Row 3: Ch 1, turn; sc in first sc, ch 1, skip next sc, ★ † working in **front** of next ch-1, dc in Front Loop Only of ch one row **below** ch-1 *(Fig. 2, page 28)*, ch 1, skip next sc †, (sc in **both** loops of next ch, ch 1, skip next sc) twice; repeat from ★ 4 times **more**, then repeat from † to † once, sc in **both** loops of last sc: 18 sts and 17 ch-1 sps.

22

Row 4: Ch 1, turn; sc in first sc, ch 1, ★ † working in **front** of next ch-1, dc in sc one row **below** ch-1, ch 1, skip next dc, working in **front** of next ch-1, dc in sc one row **below** ch-1, ch 1 †, (sc in next sc, ch 1) twice; repeat from ★ 4 times **more**, then repeat from † to † once, sc in last sc: 24 sts and 23 ch-1 sps.

Row 5: Ch 1, turn; sc in first sc, ch 1, ★ † skip next ch-1 sp, working in **front** of next ch-1, dc in dc one row **below** ch-1, ch 1, skip next dc †, (sc in next sc, ch 1) twice; repeat from ★ 4 times **more**, then repeat from † to † once, sc in last sc: 18 sts and 17 ch-1 sps.

Row 6: Ch 1, turn; sc in first sc, ch 1, ★ † working in **front** of next ch-1, dc in dc one row **below** ch-1, ch 1, skip next dc, working in **front** of next ch-1, dc in dc one row **below** ch-1, ch 1 †, (sc in next sc, ch 1) twice; repeat from ★ 4 times **more**, then repeat from † to † once, sc in last sc: 24 sts and 23 ch-1 sps.

Rows 7-32: Repeat Rows 5 and 6: 24 sts and 23 ch-1 sps.

Row 33: Ch 1, turn; sc in first sc, ch 1, ★ † skip next ch-1 sp and next dc, sc in both loops of next ch, ch 1, skip next dc and next ch-1 sp †, (sc in next sc, ch 1) twice; repeat from ★ 4 times **more**, then repeat from † to † once, sc in last sc: 18 sts and 17 ch-1 sps.

Row 34: Ch 1, turn; sc in first sc, (ch 1, sc in next sc) across; do **not** finish off.

EDGING

Rnd 1: Ch 1, do **not** turn; sc in last sc on Row 34, ch 1, working in end of rows, skip first 2 rows, (sc in next row, ch 1, skip next row) across; working in skipped chs and in free loops of beginning ch *(Fig. 1, page 28)*, (sc, ch 2, sc) in ch at base of first sc, ch 1, (skip next ch, sc in next ch, ch 1) across to last 2 chs, skip next ch, (sc, ch 2, sc) in last ch; working in end of rows, ch 1, skip first row, sc in next row, ch 1, (skip next row, sc in next row, ch 1) across to last 2 rows, skip last 2 rows; working across Row 34, (sc, ch 2, sc) in first sc, ch 1, (sc in next sc, ch 1) across, sc in same st as first sc, ch 2; join with slip st to first sc, finish off: 72 sc and 72 sps.

Rnd 2: With **wrong** side facing, join Red with sc in any corner ch-2 sp *(see Joining With Sc, page 28)*; ch 2, sc in same sp, ch 1, (sc in next ch-1 sp, ch 1) across to next corner ch-2 sp, ★ (sc, ch 2, sc) in corner ch-2 sp, ch 1, (sc in next ch-1 sp, ch 1) across to next corner ch-2 sp; repeat from ★ 2 times **more**; join with slip st to first sc, finish off.

Rnd 3: With **right** side facing, join Yellow with sc in any corner ch-2 sp; ch 2, sc in same sp, ch 1, (sc in next ch-1 sp, ch 1) across to next corner ch-2 sp, ★ (sc, ch 2, sc) in corner ch-2 sp, ch 1, (sc in next ch-1 sp, ch 1) across to next corner ch-2 sp; repeat from ★ 2 times **more**; join with slip st to first sc, finish off.

Rnds 4 and 5: Repeat Rnds 2 and 3; at end of Rnd 5; do **not** finish off.

Rnd 6: Do **not** turn; ★ (slip st, ch 2, slip st) in next ch-2 sp, ch 1, (slip st in next ch-1 sp, ch 1) across to next corner ch-2 sp; repeat from ★ around; join with slip st to first slip st, finish off.

Dishcloth #14

Shown on Back Cover.

■■■□ INTERMEDIATE

Finished Size: 10" (25.5 cm) square

MATERIALS
100% Cotton Medium Weight Yarn (MEDIUM 4)
[5 ounces, 236 yards
(140 grams, 212 meters) per ball]:
Pink - 1 ball
Yellow - 1 ball
Crochet hook, size G (4 mm) **or** size needed
for gauge
Safety pin

GAUGE SWATCH: 2¹/₂" (6.25 cm) square
Work same as Dishcloth for 3 rnds.

DISHCLOTH
Rnd 1 (Right side)**:** With Pink, ch 4, 2 dc in fourth
ch from hook **(3 skipped chs count as first dc)**,
ch 3, (3 dc in same ch, ch 3) 3 times; join with
slip st to first dc, place loop from hook onto safety
pin to prevent rnd from unraveling: 12 dc and
4 ch-3 sps.

Note: Loop a short piece of yarn around any dc to
mark Rnd 1 as **right** side.

Rnd 2: With **wrong** side facing and keeping loop
to **wrong** side of work, join Yellow with sc in any
ch-3 sp *(see Joining With Sc, page 28)*; ch 3, sc in
same sp, ch 1, skip next dc, sc in next dc, ch 1, ★ (sc,
ch 3, sc) in next ch-3 sp, ch 1, skip next dc, sc in next
dc, ch 1; repeat from ★ 2 times **more**; join with
slip st to first sc, finish off: 12 sc and 12 sps.

Rnd 3: With **right** side facing, place loop from
safety pin onto hook, ch 3 **(counts as first dc,
now and throughout)**, sc in next sc, working
behind next ch-1, dc in skipped dc one rnd **below**
ch-1, sc in next sc, ch 4, sc in next sc, ★ (working
behind next ch-1, dc in skipped dc one rnd **below**
ch-1, sc in next sc) twice, ch 4, sc in next sc; repeat
from ★ 2 times **more**; join with slip st to first dc,
place loop from hook onto safety pin to prevent rnd
from unraveling.

Rnd 4: With **wrong** side facing and keeping loop
to **right** side of work, join Yellow with sc in sc
before any ch-4 sp; ch 1, (sc, ch 3, sc) in next
ch-4 sp, ch 1, ★ sc in next sc, ch 1, (skip next dc,
sc in next sc, ch 1) across to next ch-4 sp, (sc, ch 3,
sc) in next ch-4 sp, ch 1; repeat from ★ 2 times
more, (sc in next sc, ch 1, skip next dc) twice; join
with slip st to first sc, finish off: 20 sc and 20 sps.

Rnd 5: With **right** side facing, place loop from
safety pin onto hook, ch 3, sc in next sc, working in
front of next ch-1, dc in skipped dc one rnd **below**
ch-1, sc in next sc, ★ † working **behind** next ch-1,
dc in ch-4 sp one rnd **below** ch-1 (before first sc),
sc in next sc, ch 4, sc in next sc, working **behind**
next ch-1, dc in same sp as last dc made (after
second sc), sc in next sc †, (working in **front** of
next ch-1, dc in skipped dc one rnd **below** ch-1, sc
in next sc) twice; repeat from ★ 2 times **more**, then
repeat from † to † once; join with slip st to first dc,
place loop from hook onto safety pin to prevent
rnd from unraveling: 36 sts and 4 ch-4 sps.

Rnd 6: With **wrong** side facing and keeping loop to **right** side of work, join Yellow with sc in sc **before** any ch-4 sp; ch 1, (sc, ch 3, sc) in next ch-4 sp, ch 1, ★ sc in next sc, ch 1, (skip next dc, sc in next sc, ch 1) across to next ch-4 sp, (sc, ch 3, sc) in next ch-4 sp, ch 1; repeat from ★ 2 times **more**, (sc in next sc, ch 1, skip next dc) across; join with slip st to first sc, finish off: 28 sc and 28 sps.

Rnd 7: With **right** side facing, place loop from safety pin onto hook, ch 3, sc in next sc, (working **front** of next ch-1, dc in skipped dc one rnd **below** ch-1, sc in next sc) twice, ★ † working **behind** next ch-1, dc in ch-4 sp one rnd **below** ch-1, sc in next sc, ch 4, sc in next sc, working **behind** next ch-1, dc in same sp as last dc made, sc in next sc †, (working in **front** of next ch-1, dc in skipped dc one rnd **below** ch-1, sc in next sc) 4 times; repeat from ★ 2 times **more**, then repeat from † to † once, working in **front** of next ch-1, dc in skipped dc one rnd **below** ch-1, sc in next sc; join with slip st to first sc, place loop from hook onto safety pin to prevent rnd from unraveling: 52 sts and 4 ch-4 sps.

Rnd 8: With **wrong** side facing and keeping loop to **right** side of work, join Yellow with sc in sc **before** any ch-4 sp; ch 1, (sc, ch 3, sc) in next ch-4 sp, ch 1, ★ sc in next sc, ch 1, (skip next dc, sc in next sc, ch 1) across to next ch-4 sp, (sc, ch 3, sc) in next ch-4 sp, ch 1; repeat from ★ 2 times **more**, (sc in next sc, ch 1, skip next dc) across; join with slip st to first sc, finish off: 36 sc and 36 sps.

Rnd 9: With **right** side facing, place loop from safety pin onto hook, ch 3, sc in next sc, (working in **front** of next ch-1, dc in skipped dc one rnd **below** ch-1, sc in next sc) across to within one ch-1 sp of next corner ch-4 sp, ★ † working **behind** next ch-1, dc in ch-4 sp one rnd **below** ch-1, sc in next sc, ch 4, sc in next sc, working **behind** next ch-1, dc in same sp as last dc made, sc in next sc †, (working in **front** of next ch-1, dc in skipped dc one rnd **below** ch-1, sc in next sc) across to within one ch-1 sp of next corner ch-4 sp; repeat from ★ 2 times **more**, then repeat from † to † once, (working in **front** of next ch-1, dc in skipped dc one rnd **below** ch-1, sc in next sc) across; join with slip st to first sc, place loop from hook onto safety pin to prevent rnd from unraveling: 68 sts and 4 ch-4 sps.

Rnds 10-15: Repeat Rnds 8 and 9, 3 times; at end of Rnd 15, do **not** place loop onto safety pin after joining, finish off: 116 sts and 4 ch-4 sps.

Rnd 16: With **right** side facing, join Yellow with sc in any ch-4 sp; ch 1, (sc in same sp, ch 1) 3 times, ★ skip next sc, (sc in next dc, ch 1, skip next sc) across to next ch-4 sp, (sc, ch 1) 4 times in ch-4 sp; repeat from ★ 2 times **more**, skip next sc, (sc in next dc, ch 1, skip next sc) across; join with slip st to first sc, do **not** finish off: 72 sc and 72 sps.

Rnd 17: Do **not** turn; (slip st in next ch-1 sp, ch 1) around; join with slip st to first slip st, finish off.

Dishcloth #15

Shown on Back Cover.

■■■□ INTERMEDIATE

Finished Size: 10¼" (26 cm) square

MATERIALS
100% Cotton Medium Weight Yarn **④ MEDIUM**
[5 ounces, 236 yards
(140 grams, 212 meters) per ball]:
Yellow - 1 ball
Purple - 1 ball
Crochet hook, size G (4 mm) **or** size needed
for gauge

GAUGE: 11 sts and 9 rows = 2½" (6.5 cm)

GAUGE SWATCH: 2½" (6.5 cm) square
With Yellow, ch 12.
Work same as Dishcloth for 9 rows.
Finish off.

STITCH GUIDE

> **TREBLE CROCHET** *(abbreviated tr)*
> YO twice, insert hook in sp indicated, YO and
> pull up a loop (4 loops on hook), (YO and draw
> through 2 loops on hook) 3 times.

DISHCLOTH
With Yellow, ch 36.

Row 1 (Wrong side): Sc in second ch from hook,
★ ch 1, skip next ch, sc in next ch; repeat from ★
across: 18 sc and 17 ch-1 sps.

Note: Loop a short piece of yarn around **back** of
any stitch to mark **right** side.

Rows 2 and 3: Ch 1, turn; sc in first sc, (ch 1,
sc in next sc) across.

Row 4: Ch 1, turn; sc in first sc, skip next ch-1 sp
and next sc, working in **front** of next ch-1 sp, tr in
ch-1 sp one row **below** next ch-1, sc in skipped sc,
★ (ch 1, sc in next sc) twice, skip next ch-1 sp and
next sc, working in **front** of next ch-1 sp, tr in
ch-1 sp one row **below** next ch-1 sp, sc in skipped
sc; repeat from ★ across to last sc, ch 1, sc in last sc:
24 sts and 11 ch-1 sps.

Row 5: Ch 1, turn; sc in first sc, ★ ch 1, skip next st, sc
in next sc; repeat from ★ across: 18 sc and 17 ch-1 sps.

Rows 6-34: Repeat Rows 4 and 5, 14 times; then
repeat Row 4 once **more**; do **not** finish off.

EDGING
Rnd 1: Ch 1, do **not** turn; sc in last sc on Row 34,
ch 1, skip first 2 rows, (sc in next row, ch 1, skip next
row) across; working in free loops of beginning ch
(Fig. 1, page 28), (sc, ch 2, sc) in ch at base of first
sc, ch 1, (skip next ch, sc in next ch, ch 1) across to
last 2 chs, skip next ch, (sc, ch 2, sc) in last ch; working
in end of rows, ch 1, skip first row, sc in next row,
ch 1, (skip next row, sc in next row, ch 1) across to last
2 rows, skip last 2 rows; working across Row 34, (sc,
ch 2, sc) in first sc, ch 1, (skip next st, sc in next sc,
ch 1) across, sc in same st as first sc, ch 2; join with
slip st to first sc, finish off: 72 sc and 72 sps.

Rnd 2: With **wrong** side facing, join Purple with sc
in any corner ch-2 sp **(see Joining With Sc,
page 28)**; ch 2, sc in same sp, ch 1, ★ (sc in next
ch-1 sp, ch 1) across to next corner ch-2 sp, (sc,
ch 2, sc) in corner ch-2 sp, ch 1; repeat from ★
2 times **more**, (sc in next ch-1 sp, ch 1) across; join
with slip st to first sc, finish off.

Rnd 3: With **right** side facing, join Yellow with sc
in any corner ch-2 sp; ch 2, sc in same sp, ch 1,
★ (sc in next ch-1 sp, ch 1) across to next corner
ch-2 sp, (sc, ch 2, sc) in corner ch-2 sp, ch 1; repeat
from ★ 2 times **more**, (sc in next ch-1 sp, ch 1)
across; join with slip st to first sc.

Rnd 4: Do **not** turn; ★ (slip st, ch 2, slip st) in next
ch-2 sp, ch 1, (slip st in next ch-1 sp, ch 1) across to
next corner ch-2 sp; repeat from ★ around; join with
slip st to first slip st, finish off.

26

General Instructions

ABBREVIATIONS

ch(s)	chain(s)
cm	centimeters
dc	double crochet(s)
hdc	half double crochet(s)
mm	millimeters
Rnd(s)	Round(s)
sc	single crochet(s)
sp(s)	space(s)
st(s)	stitch(es)
tr	treble crochet(s)
YO	yarn over

★ — work instructions following ★ as many **more** times as indicated in addition to the first time.

† to † — work all instructions from first † to second † **as many** times as specified.

( ) or [ ] — work enclosed instructions **as many** times as specified by the number immediately following **or** work all enclosed instructions in the stitch or space indicated **or** contains explanatory remarks.

colon (:) — the number(s) given after a colon at the end of a row or round denote(s) the number of stitches or spaces you should have on that row or round.

CROCHET TERMINOLOGY

UNITED STATES		INTERNATIONAL
slip stitch (slip st)	=	single crochet (sc)
single crochet (sc)	=	double crochet (dc)
half double crochet (hdc)	=	half treble crochet (htr)
double crochet (dc)	=	treble crochet (tr)
treble crochet (tr)	=	double treble crochet (dtr)
double treble crochet (dtr)	=	triple treble crochet (ttr)
triple treble crochet (tr tr)	=	quadruple treble crochet (qtr)
skip	=	miss

GAUGE

Exact gauge is essential for proper size. Before beginning your project, make the sample swatch given in the individual instructions in the yarn and hook specified. After completing the swatch, measure it, counting your stitches and rows or rounds carefully. If your swatch is larger or smaller than specified, **make another, changing hook size to get the correct gauge**. Keep trying until you find the size hook that will give you the specified gauge.

Yarn Weight Symbol & Names	SUPER FINE 1	FINE 2	LIGHT 3	MEDIUM 4	BULKY 5	SUPER BULKY 6
Type of Yarns in Category	Sock, Fingering Baby	Sport, Baby	DK, Light Worsted	Worsted, Afghan, Aran	Chunky, Craft, Rug	Bulky, Roving
Crochet Gauge Ranges in Single Crochet to 4" (10 cm)	21-32 sts	16-20 sts	12-17 sts	11-14 sts	8-11 sts	5-9 sts
Advised Hook Size Range	B-1 to E-4	E-4 to 7	7 to I-9	I-9 to K-10.5	K-10.5 to M-13	M-13 and larger

CROCHET HOOKS												
U.S.	B-1	C-2	D-3	E-4	F-5	G-6	H-8	I-9	J-10	K-10½	N	P	Q
Metric - mm	2.25	2.75	3.25	3.5	3.75	4	5	5.5	6	6.5	9	10	15

◼️◻️◻️◻️ BEGINNER	Projects for first-time crocheters using basic stitches. Minimal shaping.
◼️◼️◻️◻️ EASY	Projects using yarn with basic stitches, repetitive stitch patterns, simple color changes, and simple shaping and finishing.
◼️◼️◼️◻️ INTERMEDIATE	Projects using a variety of techniques, such as basic lace patterns or color patterns, mid-level shaping and finishing.
◼️◼️◼️◼️ EXPERIENCED	Projects with intricate stitch patterns, techniques and dimension, such as non-repeating patterns, multi-color techniques, fine threads, small hooks, detailed shaping and refined finishing.

HINTS

As in all crocheted pieces, good finishing techniques make a big difference in the quality of the piece. Make a habit of taking care of loose ends as you work. Thread a yarn needle with the yarn end. With **wrong** side facing, weave the needle through several stitches, then reverse the direction and weave it back through several stitches. When ends are secure, clip them off close to work.

JOINING WITH SC

When instructed to join sc, begin with a slip knot on hook. Insert hook in stitch or space indicated, YO and pull up a loop, YO and draw through both loops on hook.

JOINING WITH DC

When instructed to join sc, begin with a slip knot on hook. YO, holding loop on hook, insert hook in stitch or space indicated, YO and pull up a loop (3 loops on hook), YO and pull up a loop, (YO and draw through 2 loops on hook) twice.

FREE LOOPS OF A CHAIN

When instructed to work in free loops of a chain, work in loop indicated by arrow **(Fig. 1)**.

Fig. 1

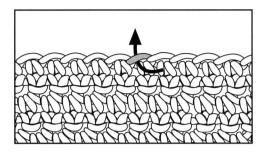

FRONT LOOP ONLY

Work only in loop(s) indicated by arrow **(Fig. 2)**.

Fig. 2

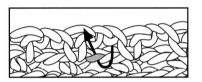

We have made every effort to ensure that these instructions are accurate and complete.
We cannot, however, be responsible for human error, typographical mistakes, or variations in individual work.

Production Team: Instructional Editor - Sarah J. Green; Technical Editor - Lois J. Long;
Graphic Artist - Ashley Carozza; and Senior Graphic Artist - Lora Puls.

Dishcloth made and instructions tested by Margaret Taverner.